For C

Enjoy!

The Power of
GRANDPARENTING

Robert Strand

Grandpa 2005

Ev|ergreen
PRESS

The Power of Grandparenting
by Robert Strand
Copyright © 2004 Robert Strand

ISBN 1-58169-156-4
For Worldwide Distribution
Printed in the U.S.A.

Evergreen Press
P.O. Box 191540 • Mobile, AL 36619

TABLE OF CONTENTS

DEDICATION

This book is dedicated to the memory of my deceased grandparents. To my Norwegian grandparents, Strand, whom I never met and to my Steen grandparents. Grandpa Steen passed away when I was three years old, and my grandmother Gina was an important influence in my youth.

And to my mother who has been a grandmother to my children and a great-grandmother to my grandchildren. (My father has been deceased and has missed out on the joys of being a great-grandfather.)

Then, there is my wife, Donna, who has become the greatest "razzle, snazzle grandma" in the whole world, according to Benjamin, age six.

INTRODUCTION

A century ago only 4% of the U.S. population even reached the age of 65, but now 12.4% of Americans are 65 and older. Life expectancy jumped to 78 years by the end of the 20th century compared to 47 years at the beginning.

According to a study by Duke University, more of these seniors are able to care for themselves. Two decades ago 26.2 % of those 65 and older had a disability that kept them from daily activities such as cooking, cleaning, or shopping. That percentage dropped to 19.7 % by the turn of the 21st century. During this same span, the number of elderly in nursing homes dropped from 6.2 % to 3.4%.

"Previous generations had to basically work until they couldn't anymore, then they were cared for by their family and then they died," says Harold Koenig, founder of the Center for the Study of Religion, Spirituality and Health at Duke University in Durham, North Carolina. "This generation, however, is retiring at a younger age and living longer after they retire," according to Koenig.

It's an unprecedented phenomenon that older adults in good health have time on their hands. Pension plans, government assistance, and self-funded retirement plans cause many to do quite well financially. "Retirement is a season to refocus.

It's a time to re-evaluate your life and to take inventory of your God-given gifts," so says Stephen Sparks.

Besides the retirees, there are many middle-aged baby boomers not yet ready to retire but who have adult children presenting them with beautiful grandbabies.

Welcome to the wonderful world of grandparenting! It's a time filled with new vistas of opportunity and challenge.

I, too, am a grandparent. In fact, eight times over, and what a delight it is! My prayer and hope is that this little book will be helpful to you in this fulfilling assignment of grandparenting. It's really grand!

Robert J. Strand
2004

CHAPTER ONE

ARE GRANDPARENTS REALLY NEEDED?

As we get older, we have a tendency to feel that our time of usefulness is swiftly passing. We need to rid ourselves of such thinking and realize that some of our most powerful work—sowing into the lives of the future generation—lies still ahead of us.

In my files I found the story of an elderly woman and her little grandson, whose face was sprinkled with bright freckles. One day they took an excursion to the local zoo that was sponsoring a face-painting artist. Lots of children were waiting in line to get their faces painted by the artist who was decorating them with tiger paws.

"You've go so many freckles, there's no place to paint!" a girl in the line teased the little fellow. Embarrassed, he dropped his head.

1

His grandmother knelt down next to him. "I love your freckles. When I was a little girl I always wanted freckles," she said, while tracing her finger across the child's cheek. "Freckles are beautiful!"

The boy looked up, "Really?"

"Of course," said the grandmother. "Why, just name me one thing that's prettier than freckles."

The little boy thought for a moment, peered intensely into his grandma's face and softly whispered, "Wrinkles."

Pretty perceptive child. The grandparent/grandchild relationship is very important to both of them and significantly adds to the level of family happiness. It's wonderful because there are lots of things for us to learn from the grandkids too. A relationship based on good communication helps us keep up with where their world is going, and sharing with grandkids gives them a larger perspective on life and a sense of being connected to past history.

According to a recent study reported in *A Consumer's Guide to Aging*, only 5% of all grandchildren see their grandparents at least twice a week and about 80% see them as little as once a year. Letters and phone calls help a lot, but there's nothing like a good visit. We need to remember that our relationship with our grandkids is always more important than anything we could ever give them. The best gift is to give of yourself to maintain and improve the grandparent/grandchild relationship.

There's another aspect of this wonderful, fulfilling relationship that should not be overlooked: We must not leave out our own children in the equation. Through our grandkids, we can become even closer to our own kids. Any previous difficulties in the relationship are easier to settle at this stage of the game since perspectives on both sides have probably changed over the years.

It's amazing how two people can begin a family and love each other through years of challenges that include financial and health problems, hurts and disappointments. Couples can grow closer together in the midst of making a living, raising children, and watching them leave the nest and have children of their own. With God's help, love can last and grow for 50 or more years in the life of a family. Love does indeed make the family go round!

Proverbs 17:6

⚡ POWER POINT: Here are some simple things that can help you create a closer relationship with your married children and their children: Don't correct your children or grandchildren, rather, affirm them. Live your life and let them live theirs. Accept and love your children and their spouses and their children. This is no time to be judgmental.

CHAPTER TWO

HOW TO BLESS YOUR GRANDKIDS

Everybody has a deep desire to be accepted by others. This desire is especially true in parental-child relationships. Receiving parental approval can have a tremendous effect on how a child's life will be lived. In fact, our relationship with our parents can also affect how we treat our kids and grandkids.

"How could anyone as dumb and ugly as you have such a good looking child?" Mark's mother was grinning as she cuddled her grandson in her arms. To most observers, her words might have been brushed aside as a bad joke; but almost instantly, they brought tears to Mark's eyes.

"Stop it!" Mark said emphatically. "That's all I've ever heard from you. It has taken me years to believe I'm not ugly and dumb. Why do you think I haven't been home in so long? I don't ever want you to call me dumb again."

Mark's mother sat in stunned silence. Tears came to her eyes. After all, she really had meant her words as a joke. But for the first time, one of her children had had the courage to confront her. For years, without realizing the impact of her words, this mother had constantly kidded her children about being stupid, fat, or ugly. After all, she had been kidded unmercifully by her mother when she was growing up... (Gary Smalley & John Trent, *The Blessing*, Thomas Nelson, Nashville, TN, 1986, p. 81).

According to Smalley and Trent, there are five essential elements that make for a powerful family blessing: 1) A meaningful touch; 2) A spoken message; 3) Attaching high value to the one being blessed; 4) Picturing a special future for the one being blessed; and 5) An active commitment to fulfill the blessing.

These five elements can be present in a casual blessing as well as in a special blessing we bestow on others.

Let me briefly share how our family has a special time of family blessing for our grandchildren. At Christmas time, with the entire family present, we honor and bless the child who has most recently turned thirteen. We gather in the living room, providing a special chair in which the child to be honored sits. First there is an explanation about the purpose for doing this, and then the blessing begins. Grandmother is first, followed by cousins or siblings who have already passed their thirteenth birthday. They are followed by aunts and uncles, and then Grandfather, who has the last and final blessing. Then the parents pray a special prayer over the child. Each of the blessings have been prepared ahead of time, and a hard copy is given to the child afterwards. (The mothers are diligent about keeping this in a special notebook for future reference and encouragement.) This has become the most powerful family time we share.

As a result, the child hears a blessing from significant people in his or her life. Their words are powerful future motivators that give them a moment they will remember for a lifetime.

For example, one time our oldest granddaughter had experienced a horrible day and went into her room and shut the door as soon as she arrived home. Eventually her mother gently knocked on her door and asked if she could come in. When she entered the room, there was the daughter, sitting in the middle of the bed with her notebook of blessings spread out in front of her. The tears were running down her face as she reaffirmed herself by reading the blessings from her personal blessing book.

Genesis 48:20

POWER POINT: A blessing can be passed on in a spontaneous, casual setting or you can make it a special event. Either way...do it! Maybe you need to pass a blessing to your own children before you bless your grandchildren. It's never too late to begin this meaningful practice.

CHAPTER THREE

MAKE GOOD MEMORIES

"People's fondest memories of family life are typically nothing really complicated nor are they expensive activities," explains Dr. Nick Stinnett in his book, *Family Building*. "They remember such things as eating meals together, going to an uncle's house together, or enjoying Dad pulling them on a sled or Mom baking cookies with them. The common thread is simply doing some things together that were enjoyable. The activities are not all entertainment; they include work, too."

Dr. Stinnett has done an extensive study of some 3000 American families, and it has led him to make this conclusion: "Strong families do a lot of activities together. They spend a great deal of time together. They work together, play together, go places together, and eat together. They are as busy as you and I or anybody else, but they make their family life a top priority with respect to the way they spend their time."

Most of our lives are crammed with activities. There are so many urgent demands that too often crowd out those things we need to do to accomplish our long term goals. We need to take time and plan our activities with our grandchildren.

There are all kinds of ways in which you can make wonderful memories for grandchildren. Use your imagination to devise once-in-a-lifetime occasions, annual celebrations, or holiday traditions, making them events that the grandchildren will look back on with a sense of happiness and joy.

To jog your creativity, think of your grandchild's birthday—make it something that says to your grandchild, "I'm happy you were born!" This is a day to celebrate! It's a day for affirming and appreciating their special identity as a part of the family of God as well as a vital part of their own family.

Think next in terms of family-get-togethers or a family reunion. These events can be times to strengthen the roots of a child. It's important for them to know about the history and magnitude of the at-large family—cousins, nieces, nephews, aunts, uncles, grandparents, as well as themselves. We need to reconnect with the past as well as connect the present and the future. At our family reunions, it's a time for family stories, pictures, jokes, memories, and songs enjoyed by the collective family, young and old alike.

Make memories around the table as you eat and talk together. We've all had too much fast-food and crazy schedules. There is nothing like a good old fashioned home cooked meal prepared by Grandma and Grandpa.

Think hard before you purchase a gift for your grandchildren. To receive a specially selected gift from a grandparent is meaningful to children. If you have run out of ideas as to what is appropriate, ask the parents for suggestions.

Walter Wangerin writes: "Let the children laugh and be glad...laugh with them, till tears run down your faces...till a memory of pure delight and precious relationship is established within them, indestructible, personal, and forever."

Ecclesiastes 3:1, 4

POWER POINT: Plan to celebrate all year long. There's always a reason to celebrate life. Think of Valentine's day, St. Patrick's Day, Easter, Mother's Day, Memorial Day, Father's Day, Fourth of July, Grandparents Day, Labor Day, Thanksgiving, Advent (the four Sundays leading up to Christmas), and always Christmas! Start some new traditions. Create innovative ways to celebrate life with your grandkids.

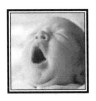

CHAPTER FOUR

GRANDPARENTING IN A CHANGING WORLD

After the birth of their first baby, Kirk and Jennifer and baby Christopher received constant care from a well-trained hospital maternity support staff. They simply had to punch the call button, and someone came running. Meals, medications, ice water, pediatric advice, breast feeding support, baby care, diaper changes, and even assistance for toilet trips for mom. This ended all too soon with the still recovering mother and nervous father waving goodbye to the discharge staff and driving off with their brand new baby strapped securely in a car seat.

What happens next? Let's look in on them. As soon as they arrive home, the new parents are immediately plunged into a different world of diapers, around-the-clock feedings, overwhelming emotions at times, and a crying baby who has trouble being pacified. Finally they tuck the newborn into his crib and quietly leave the nursery with the electronic monitor turned on. For a few moments, they are all alone.

Ten minutes later, reality hits as cries emanate from the nursery. Is he hungry? Mom has to make a quick trip to the bathroom while Dad comforts the little one. He succeeds, so they quickly decide to take advantage of the quiet and warm up their supper. They microwave a casserole a neighbor has thoughtfully brought over, and mom shakily sets the table. The phone rings, and it's Aunt Doris calling from Minnesota, who wants to hear all about the baby. Mom takes the call and keeps eating in between talking. Before the call is ended, she hears the baby crying again.

As soon as he's finished eating, Dad picks up the baby once again, but this time it doesn't work. The baby's cries get louder and more insistent. It's time to feed. Mom takes her plate with her and settles in the new rocker, thinking that maybe she could hold the baby and eat at the same time. As the baby latches on, finally the closeness and sounds of contentment bring a sense of peace and calm to them all.

Dad checks the pantry and refrigerator and asks Mom what else she needs from the store. "Be back in about an hour, honey," Dad says on the way out. As the car pulls out of the garage, Mom looks down at the peacefully sleeping baby she has just laid back in his crib, takes a deep breath, drops back into the chair, and heavily sighs...

According to author Tracy Hotchner, in her book, *Pregnancy & Childbirth: The Complete Guide for a New Life*, "The birth of a child is one of the more stressful events in a person's life." No matter how much the parents wanted the child, whether they are ready for it or not, or how positive the pregnancy and birth is, it's still an enormous upheaval in their lifestyle.

"Parents today are faced with the greatest tasks that have ever been asked of any generation," according to parent educator Dr. Donna Ewy.

So how does a new grandparent respond? We've all heard about smothering, meddling, unwelcome grandparents. How does one avoid becoming such a grandparent?

Yes, we can offer practical help (see more about this in the next chapter), but we need to also respect the new parents' preferences in the specifics. Honor their beliefs and feelings by paying attention to them as well as the baby.

Ephesians 6:7

⚡ POWER POINT: Maintain a healthy sense of humor. Do not unfavorably compare the baby to any other or your experiences to their experiences. Always respect their rules for raising their kids. And perhaps most importantly, be gracious as you help during your children's crises and also share in their joys!

CHAPTER FIVE

THE ROLE OF THE *DOULA*

Assisting new parents and grandchildren really means letting go of being the boss and becoming a servant. Further, it means knowing what to do and doing it in a quiet, cheerful manner. It also means that you give space to the new parents so they can learn by their mistakes.

Recently, a word has been used to designate the person who takes on the role of mothering-the-mother and fathering-the-father. It's the Greek word, *doula* which means the "one who serves." The doula to either or both parents could be his or her mother, a mother-in-law, a father, a father-in-law, sister, friend, spouse or professional. Whoever it is, it's usually by an invitation extended for another to come alongside during these times of adjustment with a new baby or an adopted child.

Should you be the formal or informal *doula*, you can be assured that it is a wonderful opportunity for generations to come together and create a closer bridge back through time. It's a unique opportunity to further develop the relationship. A birth can trigger powerful feelings between parents of two different generations.

New moms need to be free from some of the regular duties during the first few weeks of adjustment to the newborn. And it's precisely at these moments that the doula role is so powerful. "For at least one to two weeks (I'm not kidding)," according to Debra Evans, author and teacher of grandparenting classes, "the new mom needs to be free from cooking, cleaning, laundry, grocery shopping, errand running, church attendance, and primary care of older children, especially those under five years of age." It will be the mother's prime responsibility to rest and relax while she gets to know her new baby. This is a special "baby-moon" that needs to be set apart from regular activities so she as well as the father can focus on the new little one.

The problem is who will be there to perform these activities for her? New fathers tend to be exhausted, too, during these adjustment days and here is the opportunity for a grandparent to be a real servant, a doula in every sense of the word. And why not, the Bible even tells us to "Give her the reward she has learned!"

Galatians 6:9

⚡ POWER POINT: "At no time in history have new mothers been expected to do so much for so many with so little help," said Dr. William and Martha Sears. "Cultures around the world have always recognized the importance of mothers and babies nesting-in." When grandchildren arrive on the scene, it's time to be a real servant in every Christian sense of the word. What a role for grandparents to play! Enjoy! What pleasure! What fun!

Chapter Six

A JESUS LANDING

Howard County, Indiana, Sheriff Jerry Marr got a disturbing call one Saturday afternoon a few months ago. His six-year-old grandson Mikey had been hit by a car while fishing with his dad. The father and son were near a bridge by the Kokomo Reservoir when a woman lost control of her car, slid off the roadway, and hit Mikey at a rate of about 50 miles per hour. Sheriff Marr had seen the results of accidents like this and feared the worst. When he arrived at Saint Joseph Hospital, he rushed through the emergency room to find Mikey conscious and in fairly good spirits.

"Mikey, what happened?" Sheriff Marr asked.

Mikey replied, "Well, Papaw, I was fishin' with Dad, and some lady runned me over. I flew into a mud puddle, and broke my fishin' pole, and I didn't get to catch no fish!"

As it turned out, the impact propelled Mikey about 500 feet, over a few trees and an embankment and into the middle of a mud puddle. Miraculously, his only injuries were to his right femur bone, which had broken in two places. Mikey had surgery to place pins in his leg, but otherwise the boy was fine. Since all the boy could talk about in the emergency room was that his fishing pole was broken, the Sheriff went to the store and bought him a new one while Mikey was in surgery so he could have it when he came out. The next day the Sheriff sat with Mikey to keep him company in the hospital.

Mikey was enjoying his new fishing pole and practiced casting into the trash can as they talked about when he could go fishing again. When they were alone, Mikey matter-of-factly asked, "Papaw, did you know Jesus is real?"

"Well," the Sheriff replied, a little startled. "Yes, Jesus is real to all who believe in Him and love Him in their hearts."

"No," said Mikey. "I mean Jesus is REALLY real!"

"What do you mean?" asked the Sheriff.

"I know He's real 'cause I saw Him," said Mikey, still casting into the trash can.

"You did?" asked the Sheriff, amazed.

"Yep," said Mikey. "When that lady runned me over and broke my fishin' pole, Jesus caught me in His arms and laid me down in the mud puddle." (from *Uniting Men and Meaning*, the magazine of

United Methodist Men, Volume 5, #3, Summer 2002, p. 8).

That little boy was just as comfortable talking about Jesus with his grandfather as he was about discussing which bait to use on his next fishing trip. Part of our relationship with our grandkids is to be a spiritual nurturer to them. They need to be able to talk with us about spiritual matters.

Of course, the values we live by will make our most important impression on them. Our lives will underline, in a vivid way, the spiritual things we have shared with them. So it is important to identify the values that we want to pass on to the younger generation.

One value to pass along is to openly show them that you love the Lord Jesus Christ. Bring Him and your relationship with Him into the open where your grandkids can also get to know Him better. You do this with your words and actions.

Talking and living out that relationship should not be confined to Sunday morning or to your private devotions. Outside of church services, you need to express to them your delight in being part of the family of God and your enjoyment in being a child of the King of Kings.

Always be willing to listen and respond to any questions your grandchild will express. Make it clear that you do not think any question is stupid on their part when it comes to spiritual things.

Take the time to fully explain any answers. It always helps if you get down to their level…eye to eye. And always use any chance to help them see God in His wonderful creations.

Matthew 18:3-6

⚡ POWER POINT: Ruth Bell Graham wrote: "How many mistakes I have made with the children because I was 'fretting'…concerned to the point of worry. And invariably it prompted me to unwise action. But a mother who walks with God knows He only asks her to take care of the possible and to trust Him with the impossible; she does not need to fret." Grandma and Grandpa…are you willing to trust God with your grandchild's situations today as well as tomorrow?

Chapter Seven

A GRANDFATHER'S BLESSING

Richard Paul Evans, the author of the best-selling, *The Christmas Box*, with more than eleven million copies in print, wrote another book explaining the success of his first book. The story behind the story is contained in his more recent book, *The Christmas Box Miracle*, which he calls, "My spiritual journey of destiny, healing and hope."

One of the life-changing events affecting his life journey came to him in the form of a blessing given to him by his grandfather. Let's pick up some of his memories of what happened:

"At some point every one of my siblings received a blessing from my grandfather. They were not all healing blessings…rather they were similar to the kind written about in the Old Testament, as when Isaac blessed his son Jacob. Every blessing given to us was unique and spoke to us individually of the journey we would walk on this earth. Most of my grandfather's blessings were counsels on how to live righteously, though portions were prophetic of the challenges and opportunities that would come to us.

"One afternoon, shortly after I had turned twelve, I went with my parents to my grandfather's house. After talking with me for a short while, my grandfather laid his hands on my head and began to speak. Among the many words of blessing, he told me that someday I would 'walk with the royalty of this earth and be known as one who loves God.'" (Richard Paul Evans, *The Christmas Box Miracle*, Simon & Schuster, New York, 2002, p 44)

Richard Evans' blessing had been recorded on an old reel-to-reel tape recorder and transcribed by his grandmother. When it was printed out and given to him, he glued it inside the cover of one of his journals for further reference. The spoken blessing is powerful, but a blessing, which is spoken as well as written, will stay with a grandchild for the rest of his life. What a powerful behavior modifier for a child!

When we receive a blessing, we receive not only the approval all of us need, but also the encouragement to really make an effort in life. It raises our expectations and lifts up our standard for what we demand of ourselves.

Children and teens need grandparents because they are in the period of life when they are developing their own identity. They are seeking independence from their parents, yet they need adults in their life whom they love and trust. They need all kinds of advice from grandparents, even though they may not recognize it. Therefore, advice for their future can often be shared in the form of a blessing.

Today, the size of families is diminishing. Children don't have as many siblings as families of yesteryears, and the number of single-parent homes are increasing. In such a world grandparents are needed more than ever. One powerful way of staying connected to grandchildren is by way of giving them a blessing.

Oh, yes, his grandfather's blessing has come to pass for Richard Evans. He wrote: "...I have met actors, directors, authors, diplomats, political leaders, renowned journalists, religious leaders, athletes and sports legends, billionaires and business magnates. We have eaten lunch at the home of President George and Mrs. Barbara Bush. I have shared the podium with President George W. Bush and first lady Laura Bush. I have visited with former British prime minister John Major and eaten breakfast with Elizabeth Dole.

"My grandfather's words have come true. I have indeed walked with the royalty of this earth" (*ibid*, pp 251-252).

Proverbs 10:6

⚡ POWER POINT: Grandparents have a unique position of trust with their grandchildren. From that vantage point, they have the power of wisdom and can pass along a fabulous look into the future for their grandkids. Try it! You might be amazed at the long-term results!

Chapter Eight

WHAT DO I SAY IN A BLESSING?

Perhaps you've been thinking, "I'd like to start blessing my kids and grandkids, but what specifically can I say?" Well, I'm glad you asked. Here are at least 30 things from the Bible, which you can say in blessing others:

God bless you with ability.

God bless you with abundance.

God bless you with clear direction.

God bless you with the protection of angels.

God bless you with the assurance of His love and His grace.

God bless you with a controlled and disciplined life.

God bless you with courage.

God bless you with creativity.

God bless you with spiritual perception of His truth.

God bless you with ever increasing faith.

God bless you with His favor and with the favor of others.

God bless you with good health.

God bless you with a good spouse.

God bless you with the desire to bless others with your hands.

God bless you with fulfilling happiness.

God bless you with contentment.

God bless you with hope and a good outlook on all of life.

God bless you with a listening ear for others.

God bless you with a long and fulfilled life.

God bless you with an obedient heart to the Spirit of God.

God bless you with His peace.

God bless you with pleasant speech.

God bless you with a pleasing personality.

God bless you with favor and promotion in your life's calling.

God bless you with protection from all who would harm you.

God bless you with promotions.

God bless you with provision, safety and strength.

God bless you with success in all you do.

God bless you with trust and His wisdom.

God bless you with goodness and mercy following you all the days of your long and fruitful life so that you can dwell in His house forever!

When you bless others, you are both affirming them and encouraging them. When Jesus blessed His followers with such statements as, "You are the light of the world, you are the salt of the earth…" they really had not yet attained such a position at the time, but they eventually rose to the level of their blessing.

We should never withhold the blessing when it's in our power to give it! Everybody goes through life seeking for approval, and this approval is especially important when it comes from family members who know us probably better than most.

The following scriptural passage is a wonderful blessing that the Lord told Moses to pass along:

Tell Aaron and his sons, "This is how you are to bless the Israelites. Say to them: 'The Lord bless you and keep you; the Lord make his face shine upon you and be gracious to you; the Lord turn his face towards you and give you peace.'" So they will put my name on the Israelites, and I will bless them (Numbers 6:22-27).

POWER POINT: Did you notice the above blessing is the means of "marking" the Israelites for God? "So they will put my name on them." What a powerful way to mark your special loved ones. Put the name of God on them. Mark them with your blessings of love! Honor them! Raise their life expectations!

(If you desire to do a more complete study on the blessing, I highly recommend this book, *The Blessing*, Gary Smalley & John Trent, Thomas Nelson Publishers, Nashville, TN, 1986. Also, there is a special workbook available to be used in conjunction with it.)

CHAPTER NINE

101 WORDS THAT WILL BLESS YOUR GRANDKIDS

When we share a word of encouragement, praise, acceptance, or blessing with our grandchildren, it helps when we use words that they can relate to easily. If we do it often, we will see what a significant difference it can make in their lives.

Make these words become part of your thinking and vocabulary and let them be a response, especially when the child least expects it. There are too many kids who go through life seeking and hoping for approval. Don't withhold it when it is in your power to speak it.

WOW…WAY TO GO…SUPER…
YOU'RE SPECIAL…OUTSTANDING…
EXCELLENT…GREAT…GOOD…
NEAT…WELL DONE…REMARKABLE…

I KNEW YOU COULD DO IT...
I'M PROUD OF YOU...FANTASTIC...
SUPER STAR... NICE WORK...
LOOKING GOOD...YOU'RE ON TOP OF IT...
BEAUTIFUL...NOW YOU'RE FLYING...
YOU'RE CATCHING ON...
NOW YOU'VE GOT IT...
YOU'RE INCREDIBLE...BRAVO...
YOU'RE FANTASTIC...
HURRAY FOR YOU...
YOU'RE ON TARGET...HOW NICE...
HOW SMART...GOOD JOB...
THAT'S INCREDIBLE...HOT DOG...
DYNAMITE...YOU'RE BEAUTIFUL...
YOU'RE UNIQUE...
NOTHING CAN STOP YOU NOW...
GOOD FOR YOU...I LIKE YOU...
YOU'RE A WINNER...
REMARKABLE JOB...
BEAUTIFUL WORK...SPECTACULAR...
YOU'RE SPECTACULAR...
YOU'RE DARLING...YOU'RE PRECIOUS...
GREAT DISCOVERY...
YOU'VE DISCOVERED THE SECRET...
YOU FIGURED IT OUT...
FANTASTIC JOB...HIP, HIP, HURRAY...
BINGO...MAGNIFICENT...MARVELOUS...
TERRIFIC...YOU'RE IMPORTANT...
PHENOMENAL...YOU'RE SENSATIONAL...

SUPER WORK…CREATIVE WORK…
SUPER JOB…
EXCEPTIONAL PERFORMANCE…
YOU'RE A REAL TROOPER…
YOU ARE RESPONSIBLE…
YOU ARE EXCITING…
YOU LEARNED IT RIGHT…
WHAT AN IMAGINATION…
WHAT A GOOD LISTENER…
YOU ARE FUN…YOU'RE GROWING UP…
YOU TRIED HARD…YOU CARE…
BEAUTIFUL SHARING…
OUTSTANDING PERFORMANCE…
YOU'RE A GOOD FRIEND…
I TRUST YOU…YOU'RE IMPORTANT…
YOU MEAN A LOT TO ME…
YOU MAKE ME HAPPY…
YOU BELONG…YOU'VE GOT A
FRIEND…YOU MAKE ME LAUGH…
YOU BRIGHTEN MY DAY…
I RESPECT YOU…
YOU MEAN THE WORLD TO ME…
THAT'S CORRECT…YOU'RE A JOY…
DELIGHTFUL…
YOU'RE A TREASURE…
YOU'RE WONDERFUL…YOU'RE PERFECT…
AWESOME…A+ JOB…YOU'RE A-OKAY…
MY BUDDY…YOU MADE MY DAY…
THAT'S THE BEST…A BIG HUG…
A BIG KISS…

And always do not forget this one: I LOVE YOU!!

One more thing to remember: A smile is an unspoken blessing that is worth a thousand words or more!

Proverbs 10:21a

⚡ POWER POINT: There is now no excuse because you can't find the right words at the right moment. You may be thinking that your own parents never blessed you with such words. Maybe because you have been a victim of this spoken neglect, you have been treating your children and grandchildren in the same way. It's time to break the cycle of silence! Begin today by sharing a verbal word of encouragement.

Chapter Ten

LEAVING A LEGACY

Have you read the old Greek myth of Charon, the kindly boatman whose job it was to ferry spirits of the departed across the river Styx into the future world? When a woman came to be carried across, Charon reminded her that she might drink of the waters of Leathe and forget all her past. The woman exclaimed, "I shall drink and forget all that I have suffered!"

"Yes," the boatman told her, "and all that you have enjoyed."

"I shall drink and forget all of my failures!"

"And, all of your victories," he said.

"I shall drink and forget all who have hated me!"

"And, all who have loved you."

After a little thought, the woman entered Charon's boat without drinking the waters of forgetfulness.

We can choose our memories by thoughtfully planning them. When we leave special memories behind, they are irreplaceable legacies for our grandchildren.

Your grandchildren will also appreciate having something tangible of Grandma's or Grandpa's to remind them of their unique relationship and heritage. Think in terms of a family archive. Make a record of family history, which will probably entail some effort and lots of hard work, but will be priceless in their eyes. For example, you can compile scrapbooks, videos, pictures, CDs, family movies, memory albums, keepsake boxes, or a tracing of the family tree that you can give to them.

Then there's the spiritual legacy that you can leave them. You might ask yourself, "Do I talk frequently with my grandchildren about the Lord? Have I introduced them to the beauty of His presence and the glory of His creative genius? Have I shared with them the delight in His abundant blessings? Years from now, will they be walking with the Lord following in the footprints I leave behind?"

Make it a point to "grandparent on purpose." Our special relationship with our grandchildren springs out of the knowledge that time is quickly passing. We may or may not see our grandchildren grow up, marry, and have children of their own. The day is coming when we shall depart this world, but until then, we must take every advantage that time offers us to bless the next generation. We still have much to offer and, in turn, receive from our grandchildren.

Have you considered leaving a monetary legacy as well? Many of us might outlive our "retirement" nest egg, but even a small inheritance will be of help. Consider this admonition, "A good man (or woman) leaves an inheritance for his children's children…" (Proverbs 13:22). When making out your will, don't forget your children's children, even though it may only be passing on to them some special art object or a piece of furniture.

When we are long gone, what will we have left behind for our grandchildren to pass along to their grandchildren? How will they remember us? Lasting legacies are not carved in marble monuments…but in a life fully lived out and shared with others. Hodding Carter put it like this: "There are only two lasting bequests we can hope to give our children (and grandchildren), one of these is roots; the other is wings."

Psalm 90:12

POWER POINT: Grandparents are so blessed in that we have this wonderful opportunity to share ourselves with this new generation of God's children. My prayer is that we realize how fleeting these moments with our grandchildren actually are and make the most of them.

CHAPTER ELEVEN

BECOMING BETTER GRANDPARENTS

How do we become the kind of grandparents that will make an impact on future generations? In the remaining chapters of this book, we'll take a look at who we are, where we have come from, and what we can do that will determine the influence we will have in the future.

Who are we? As grandparents we have to first of all understand that we are survivors of one of the most tumultuous periods in history and have witnessed more change than any other previous generation! Let's consider just a few of the changes we have witnessed in our lifetimes:

We were born before all-day television (how many of us watched the test pattern, waiting for programming to begin?), frozen foods, Xerox, contact lenses, frisbees, credit cards, laser beams, ball point pens, pantyhose, dishwashers, clothes dryers, electric blankets, air conditioners, personal computers, cell phones, fax machines, the internet and e-mail, plastic packaging, palm pilots, MTV, and before anybody even thought about walking on the moon or living in a space capsule! In our time, rabbits were not cars, and designer jeans were scheming girls in our French class.

We thought fast food was what you ate during Lent and outer space was the back of the Bijou Theater. We came before house-husbands, computer dating, dual careers, day care centers, group therapy, and nursing homes. We never heard of FM or satellite radio, tape decks, CDs, VCRs, artificial hearts, word processors, yogurt, satellite dishes, picture phones, and guys wearing earrings. For us, time sharing meant togetherness, not condominiums, a "chip" meant a piece of wood, hardware meant nails, screws, and door hinges, and software wasn't even a word.

When we were young, "Made in Japan" meant junky merchandise and not slick cars. Pizza, McDonalds, Wendys, Burger King, Starbucks, Krispy Kreme, and instant coffee were unheard of.

We hit the scene when there were five and dime stores, where you actually bought things for five and ten cents. The local soda shop sold ice cream cones for a nickel or a dime. For one nickel you could ride a streetcar, make a phone call, buy a Coke, or enough stamps to mail one letter and two post-cards. You could buy a new Chevy or Ford coupe for about $600, but who could afford one? A pity, too, because gas was eleven cents a gallon! In our day rock music was Grandma's lullaby and aids were helpers. When in church we had song services and sang out of hymn books and not off the wall in worship services.

Not only are we survivors of these "primitive" conditions, but we are happy, excited, healthy and living longer than previous generations of grandparents. Our unique perspective allows us to build a bridge to future generations.

Psalm 39

⚡ POWER POINT: Deeply spiritual people live longer because of a "helper's high." When we are helpful in meeting the needs of others and not expecting anything in return, it produces a euphoria that we know we've made a difference in the life of others. And we have much to give! Just look at our history! We are survivors!

CHAPTER TWELVE

A LESSON ON LIVING

On the first day of college classes, our professor introduced himself and challenged us to get to know someone we didn't already know. I stood up to look around when a gentle hand touched my shoulder. I turned around to find a wrinkled, little old lady beaming up at me with a smile that lit up her entire being.

She said, "Hi, handsome. My name is Rose. I'm 87 years old. Can I give you a hug?"

I laughed and enthusiastically responded, "Of course you may," and she gave me a giant squeeze.

"Why are you in college at such a young, innocent age?" I asked.

She jokingly replied, "I'm here to meet a rich husband, get married, and have a couple of kids…"

"No, seriously," I asked. I was curious about her motivation at her age.

"I always dreamed of having a college education, and now I'm getting one!" she told me.

Over the course of the year, Rose became a campus icon and easily made friends wherever she went. She was something special. She was enjoying life and living it up. At the end of the semester, we invited Rose to be the speaker at our year-end football banquet. I'll never forget what she taught all of us.

She was introduced and stepped to the podium. As she began to deliver her prepared speech, she dropped her three-by-five cards on the floor. Frustrated and a bit embarrassed, she leaned into the microphone and simply said, "I'm sorry I'm so jittery. I gave up beer for Lent and this whiskey is killing me! I'll never get my speech back in order, so let me just tell you what I know." We laughed and she cleared her throat and began again:

"We do not stop playing because we are old; we grow old because we stop playing. There are only four secrets to staying young, being happy, and achieving success. 1) You have to laugh and find humor in every day. 2) You have to have a dream. When you lose your dreams, you die. 3) There is a huge difference between growing older and growing up. Anybody can grow older. The idea is to grow up by always finding the opportunity to change. 4) Have no regrets. The elderly usually don't have regrets for what they did, but rather for things they did not do. The only people who fear death are those with regrets."

She concluded her speech by courageously singing, "The Rose." She challenged each of us to study the lyrics and live them out. At the year's end, Rose completed the college degree she had begun so many years ago.

One week after graduation, Rose died peacefully in her sleep. More than 2000 college students attended her funeral in tribute to the wonderful woman who taught by example that it's never too late to be all you can possible be! (Rose Hodgin, *The Pastor's Story File*, Vol. 20, #2, Platteville, CO, adapted)

Proverbs 8:17-19

POWER POINT: Growing older is a non-negotiable mandatory part of life. Although growing up into maturity is optional, it's entirely necessary if we want true happiness and fulfillment.

CHAPTER THIRTEEN

BUT, I AM ONLY…

Have you been guilty of hiding behind the excuse, "I am only a senior citizen?" Be honest…have you? Or maybe your excuse sounds like this, "I am only one person" or "I am only a one-talent person?" It's a very human tendency to excuse our inactivity or lack of action. Well, let's take a closer look at this subject.

The *Wall Street Journal*, carried the interesting story about Harry Lipsig, who at 88 years young, decided to build a new law firm. He had worked for over 60 years in a New York law firm helping build their clientele, now he was going to start a new firm by himself. The first case was a bit unusual…here it is:

A lady was bringing suit against the city of New York because one of their police officers was driving while drunk in a squad car, which struck and killed her 71-year-old husband. Her argument was that the city had deprived her of her husband's future earnings potential. The city attorneys countered back with their argument that at the age of 71, he had little or no earnings potential. They thought they had a clever defense, until it dawned on them that this lady's argument about her husband's future potential was being advanced by a vigorous 88-year-old attorney! The city of New York settled out of court for $1.25 million!

Now what if Harry Lipsig had said, "I'm only a senior citizen?"

Our attitudes are the results of the choices we make—we can be a senior in age and still make a difference in the lives of others. Talking about choice...

Back when the Romans were the number one world power, there was a Roman general who had a unique way in which he dealt with a spy. When a spy was caught, tried in the courtroom of military justice, and stood convicted before the general, the general asked him, "What will you choose—the execution squad or the black door?" The convicted man's choice was inevitably the execution squad.

One day, a convicted spy who had chosen the execution squad was led away, and the sounds of his judgment carried back into the room where the general and his aide were sitting.

"General," the aide asked, "what is behind the black door that no condemned man ever chooses?"

"Freedom," the General answered, "but few men have the courage to choose the unknown, even over sure death."

Let's make more of the right attitudinal choices! No longer will we say, "I am only a..." Instead we need to choose freedom, choose to be involved, choose to make a difference, choose to help others, choose to be productive, choose to be positive, choose to love, choose to be joyful—in other words, choose to make better choices!

The bottom line is that an attitude of "I am only..." is not pleasing to God!

Jeremiah 1:7-8

⚡ POWER POINT: I don't have any idea about how old Jeremiah was at the time of this most fascinating exchange. He said I can't do what you are asking me to because "I am only a child." Notice that excuse didn't hold water with God who replied, "Do not say, 'I am only...'!" In the original, this is a powerful "do not"! Further, God said, "Do not be afraid" and He supplied what Jeremiah had said he lacked. God is prepared to help you overcome your "I am only..." complex! Will you allow Him to help?

CHAPTER FOURTEEN

IT'S ALL IN YOUR ATTITUDE

The Rev. Don Shelby was preaching a sermon, and he used the following personal illustration:

"Extravagances and luxuries did not exist for my mother. The one exception to her frugality was a frilly nightgown which she had never worn. She explained, 'I have that nightgown so that if I ever have to go to the hospital, I'll still look nice.'

"Years later, my mother began to suffer from a mysterious disease which destroyed her health and vitality. On a winter's day before her 69th birthday, she packed up her nightgown and checked into the hospital for tests.

"The physician confided with me over the final test results: my mother had only a matter of weeks to live. I agonized for days over whether to tell her the news. Was there any hope I could give her?

"I decided not to tell her...not just yet. I resolved instead to lift her spirits on her birthday by giving her the most expensive and beautiful matching nightgown and robe I could find. At the very least, I thought, she would feel like the prettiest lady in the hospital, dignified as she lay dying.

"After unwrapping the present, my mother said nothing. Finally, pointing to the gift on her bed, she asked, 'Would you mind returning it to the store? I don't really want it.' She then picked up a newspaper and pointing to an ad for a summertime designer purse, and explained, 'This is what I really want.' Why would my ever frugal mother want an expensive summer purse in the middle of winter when she couldn't even use it until June? She probably wouldn't even live to see spring, much less summer.

"Then I realized that my mother was asking me how long I thought she would live—in other words, would she make it to summer. Thinking it over later, I decided that perhaps if I thought she'd live long enough to use the purse, maybe she really would. When I brought the purse to her hospital bed, she held it tightly against her, with a smile on her face.

"Many years later, that particular purse is long worn out, as are half a dozen others. Next week my mother celebrates her 83rd birthday, and she is still going strong! My gift to her? The most expensive designer purse I can find. Oh, yes, she will use it well!" (Don Shelby in a sermon, *Where God Can Be Seen*, adapted)

Right! It's in attitude! It's amazing what can and will happen with the right attitude in living. Of course that's not the only reason why our lives are long or short, but it greatly affects how we live and how we die.

I was visiting a member of my church, standing by his bedside, when the attending surgeon came into the room. He immediately recognized me and said, "I'm so glad to see you here, Reverend. It really helps my patients to have a good support system. The people who pray recover sooner, and I've found they live longer than people who don't pray!" Now that's not scientific but a personal observation from a doctor/surgeon. It's in your attitude!

Philippians 4:8

POWER POINT: Anais Nin said, "We don't see things as they are, we see them as we are." It's never too late to have a check-up from the neck-up! Aging is no excuse for continuing to live with a lousy attitude. By improving our attitude we even make life more comfortable for those with whom we love and care about. Even your grandkids will detect the difference!

CHAPTER FIFTEEN

OVERCOMING LIFE'S OBSTACLES

From your perspective of life as a grandparent, no doubt you have made some discoveries about the philosophy of life. One such lesson might be that life is not always easy, wouldn't you agree? In fact, for most of us, life has not been fair and certainly there have been difficulties, trials, and tests along the way. Many of the world's leaders and achievers have been saddled with disabilities and adversities but have managed to overcome them.

The real question might be: Were these people leaders and achievers or did their overcoming the difficulties make them great? Consider…

Cripple a man, and you have a Sir Walter Scott.

Lock him in a prison cell, take away his freedom, take him out of circulation, and you have a John Bunyan.

Bury him in the snows of Valley Forge, facing an enemy which far outnumbered his troops, and you have a George Washington.

Raise him in abject poverty, make him struggle through political defeat after defeat, let him lose the love of his life, make him ugly, and you have an Abraham Lincoln.

Subject him to a difficult up-bringing, expose him to bitter religious prejudice, and you have a Disraeli.

Strike him down with infantile paralysis, take away his legs, make him dependent completely on others, and he becomes a Franklin Roosevelt.

Burn him so severely in a schoolhouse fire that the medical people say he will never walk again, and you have a man who never gave up until in 1934 he ran the world's record mile, and you have created a Glenn Cunningham.

Deafen a musical genius composer, and you have made a Ludwig van Beethoven.

Have him or her born black into a society filled with racial discrimination, and you have a Booker T. Washington, a Harriet Tubman, a Marion Anderson, a George Washington Carver, a Martin Luther King, Jr., or a Nelson Mandela.

Make him the first child in an Italian family of 18 children, subject him to grinding poverty, gift him musically, and you have an Enrico Caruso.

Have him born of parents who managed to survive a Nazi concentration camp, paralyze him from the waist down when he is aged four, and you have an incomparable concert violinist, Itzhak Perlman.

Call him a slow learner, tab him as being retarded, write him off as being uneducable, and you have an Albert Einstein.

Ban him to an island prison, age him, give him visitors, and you have a John the Beloved.

Give him the world's most unusual birth, let him be ridiculed by the religious establishment of his day, crucify him in an agonizing death, and you have Jesus Christ!

When looking back on the challenges of life, remember the challenging circumstances that put backbone in you were the things that forever changed what you would become. Thank God for them and share about them from time to time with your grandchildren.

Philippians 4:13

⚡ POWER POINT: You, as a grandparent, must develop, if you already don't have it, an enthusiasm for life that is contagious to your children and grandchildren! What a legacy to leave them! You can inspire them in spite of any obstacles which have come your way. You are not only a survivor, you are an overcomer!

Chapter Sixteen

JOY AND LAUGHTER

C an you remember a time when your life was more joyful and laughter filled? A recent study found that children laugh an average of 100 to 150 times a day while adults laugh only about 10 times a day! What's happened to us? We have a laughter famine, especially in the church. We need to laugh at ourselves and with others much more frequently than we do! Jesus was obviously the most joyful person who ever walked this earth because the Bible says that, "Therefore God, your God, has set you above your companions by anointing you with the oil of joy!" (Hebrews 1:9)

Contemporary novelist John Updike described his parents as "inclined to laugh a lot and examine everything for the fingerprints of God."

Laughter is one of those good gifts from God! Most of us tend to live life dead-pan and grim. We tackle too many of life's problems head-on without the release of laughter, ignoring the fact that it's good for your liver! Research has proven that to be true.

In that spirit, let me share with you a story about a grandmother and her granddaughter, a precocious ten-year-old. They were spending the day together when the little girl suddenly looked up and asked, "How old are you, Grandma?"

The grandmother was a bit startled but knowing her granddaughter's quick little mind, she wasn't too shocked. "Well, honey, when you're my age you don't share your age with anybody."

"Aw, go ahead, Grandma...you can trust me!"

"No, dear, I never tell anyone my age."

Then, Grandma got busy fixing dinner and suddenly realized the little darling had been absent for about 20 minutes...much too long! She checked and found the girl upstairs in Grandma's bedroom. Her granddaughter had dumped the contents of her purse on top of the bed and was sitting in the middle of the mess, holding her grandmother's driver's license.

When their eyes met, the child announced, "Grandma, you're 76!"

"Why, yes, I am. How did you know that?"

"I found the date of your birthday here on your driver's license and subtracted that year from this year...so, you're 76!"

"That's right, sweetheart. Your grandmother is 76."

The little girl continued, staring at the driver's license and added, "You also made an 'F' in sex, Grandma!"

Ever feel that somewhere between childhood innocence and today, life has become too grim? When did a well exercised sense of humor and joy get sacrificed on the altar of adulthood? Who says that being a Christian means you must have a long face? To be joyful is a choice! To laugh is a choice!

Some of God's choicest servants have been joyful people. Take Oswald Chambers, the man who wrote one of the best devotional books of all time, *My Utmost For His Highest*. He was known and loved for his rollicking sense of humor. After meeting Chambers for the first time, one serious young seminary student said: "I was shocked at what I then considered his undue levity. He was the most irreverent Reverend I had ever met!"

Charles Spurgeon, famous for his writing and preaching, was rebuked by a lady in his congregation for too much humor in his preaching, to which he replied, "Madame, you should give me a medal for holding it back as much as I do."

Laughter is good for what ails us.

Habakkuk 3:17-18

POWER POINT: Are you aware that the words "joy", "joyful" or "joyfully" appear more than 200 times in the Bible? The word "laugh" is found 40 some times! The word "rejoice" 248 times! Do you need strength? It's found in the "joy" of the Lord!

CHAPTER SEVENTEEN

MORE LAUGHTER

Are you concerned about your health and desire to get your body in better shape? Here's a laugh prescription according to Dr. William Fry, psychiatrist at Stanford Medical School: "Laugh 100 times a day and you may feel like an idiot, but you'll be in great shape. In fact, you'll have given your heart the same workout you'd get if you pedaled on a stationary bike for 15 minutes. Over time, chuckling this much also lowers blood pressure and heart rate, reduces pain, strengthens the immune system, and cuts down on stress-creating hormones. The biggest problem is finding that many things to laugh about."

To get you started, let me tell you two stories. An older couple had married, lived, and raised their family in Houston, Texas. Now they were approaching retirement age and deciding where they would make their retirement home. All of their children had moved away to different parts of the country and one son was living overseas. After much deliberation, they finally decided that it would be best to move near their only daughter and her family who happened to live in St. Cloud, Minnesota.

They shopped for a nice comfortable home and selected one, moving in during the later months of summer. They had never experienced a Minnesota winter, so they both were quite eager for this new adventure.

One winter morning, while eating breakfast, they were listening to the local news when the announcer said: "We are having a snowstorm that will dump up to ten inches of snow today. You will need to park your car on the even-numbered side of the street so the snowplows can clear your street. The snow ordinance is in effect until the storm is over." The wife immediately went out and moved the car to the even-numbered side of the street.

A week later, while eating breakfast, the radio announcer again said: "We are expecting that this storm will leave about eight inches today. You must park your car on the odd-numbered side of the street so the snowplows can clear the streets. The snow ordinance is in effect until the storm is over." Again, the wife moved their car to the odd-numbered side of the street. The husband sat and watched her do this little chore.

Two weeks later they were eating breakfast once more while listening to the morning news. The announcer broke into the regular programming with this announcement: "We are expecting between 15 and 20 inches of snow with the current storm. The snow ordinance will be in effect today and until the storm blows over. You will need to park your car..." At this instant, the electrical power went out.

The wife was really upset and shrieked, "I don't know what to do! Which side of the street do I need to park on so the plows can get through? And furthermore, for that matter, why am I the only one who always has to move the car when it snows?"

The husband didn't seem terribly upset or concerned about his wife's outburst. He simply poured himself another cup of coffee and calmly answered: "Perhaps we should just leave the car in the garage this time."

Can you stand another one? Well, anyway, here goes. A retired couple were having another argument about who should brew the coffee each morning for their breakfast.

She said, "You should do it because you get up first, and you wouldn't have to wait as long to get your coffee."

He said, "You are in charge of the cooking, you should do it and I will wait for my coffee."

She countered, "No, you should because the Bible says the men are to do the coffee."

He responded, "I can't believe that. Show me."

She pulled down their Bible, opened to the New Testament and showed him at the top of several pages, that it indeed says: "HE BREWS!"

Proverbs 15:13

⚡ POWER POINT: Go to your library or bookstore and find some funny books. Rent an old classic funny movie, have some friends over, and laugh till your side hurts.

CHAPTER EIGHTEEN

LET'S TAKE TIME
TO SOLVE A PUZZLE

One of the ways in which to keep young is to keep on challenging your thinking by playing games, reading, enrolling in some classes, volunteering at a local hospital, or a myriad of other things available for us to do.

In the spirit of keeping our minds young, I am including the following brain teaser. It was supposedly created by a grandmother named Lucy who responded to a challenge proposed by a man from Philadelphia. He was offering a reward of $1,000 to anyone who could write a biblical puzzle he could not solve. She wrote the puzzle, submitted it, and because he failed to solve it, she was awarded the $1,000 prize. Here is what Grandma Lucy wrote:

Adam, God made out of dust,
   but He thought it best to make me first.

So I was made before man,
   to answer God's most holy plan.
A living being I became,
   and Adam gave to me my name.
I from his presence then withdrew,
   and more of Adam never knew.
I did my Maker's law obey,
   nor ever went from it astray.
Thousands of miles I go in fear,
   but seldom on earth appear.
For purpose wise which God did see,
   He put a living soul in me.
A soul from me God did claim,
   and took from me the soul again.
So when from me the soul had fled,
   I was the same as when first made.
And without hands or feet or soul,
   I travel on from pole to pole.
I labor hard by day, by night,
   to fallen man I give great light.
Thousands of people, young and old,
   will by my death great light behold.

No right or wrong I can conceive.
   The Scripture I cannot believe.
Although my name therein is found,
   They are to me an empty sound.
No fear of death doth trouble me.
   Real happiness I'll never see.

To heaven I shall never go,
    Or to hell below.
Now when these lines you slowly read,
    Go search your Bible with all speed.
For that my name is written there,
    I do honestly to you declare.
WHO AM I?

Okay…I'll confess, it took me about twenty minutes to figure this out. But showing this to a granddaughter, she figured it out in about two minutes. Don't give up. It's an excellent exercise to stir up some of that gray matter between our ears.

Hebrews 12:1b

⚡ POWER POINT: William B. Terhune once said, "If one would understand older people, one should first age." "Oldness" is not reaching certain birthdays…it's much more. It's the changing of priorities that are physical, mental, social, and economic. For a person who has formed good habits of living and the adjustments to inevitable changing circumstances, life continues to be an exciting adventure. Growth should continue during the sixties, seventies, eighties and beyond, much like it did in youth!

PS: The answer to the riddle is found on page 87! If you haven't figured it out, why not run it by your grandkids?

CHAPTER NINETEEN

FREEDOM!

On the day of his retirement, so the story goes, James Chamberlain, of London, England, took to work the trusty alarm clock which had roused him out of his sleep at 5:30 am each morning for the past 47 years. He placed this alarm clock in the 80-ton steel press he had operated for all those years and roared the word "Freedom!" over the noise of the factory for all to hear as he smashed the infernal waker-upper with relish.

Freedom...what a wonderful feeling and emotion! We were born seeking it. Perhaps you also noticed that as soon as your children were born, they began the quest for freedom. They kicked and screamed at every kind of restraint. They wanted out of their cribs, their car seats, the playpens, the nursery, and then out of the house, the yard, the playground, and school, and especially parental control.

The search continues. All of us were convinced that if we could just leave home, freedom would be ours. The search goes on through promotions on the job and up the ladder of life—always with us in search of that elusive thing called freedom.

Sadly, most of us discovered that the more successful we became, the less freedom it allowed us to enjoy. Then, suddenly, aging brings retirement and freedom, although not complete freedom, because we never reach that plateau. A retired friend said, "Bob, do you know what I really like about retirement?" He didn't even wait for my reply but continued, "If there's something I have to do, I don't have to do it!"

The alarm clock can be smashed; early morning commuter traffic jams can be avoided; no more time clocks to punch; day-timers can be ignored; sales schedules are thrown away; there are no more committee meetings or trustees to deal with! The freedoms we desire and find (with limitations) is not only a freedom" from," it should be a freedom "to" and "for"!

We should not simply crawl into a vacuum, but move into things that are more desirable, more productive, and more pleasurable. Our priorities should change! This is true at every level of life. Our priorities as a child or teen are much different than those we currently have set. This freedom we now have is not a freedom just to be free. It's a freedom that allows us to be free to set different priorities!

Let others take that trip down ulcer street; let others pick up the burdens of the rat race; allow somebody else to take your place in the daily dog-eat-dog-fight. Peter Schwed wrote: "When you give up power and authority, you also give up the headaches, the pressures, and the ulcers that so frequently go with it…the bus is much less crowded in the rear."

However, that said, it's time to set new priorities. Freedom that comes in "retirement" will not be ours because we simply avoid all responsibilities, but it will now be possible to take on new assignments that are appropriate to our senior years.

The Shakers had a verse for this time in life:

> Leave the flurry
> To the masses;
> Take your time
> And shine your glasses.

Freedom from the daily grind is really a license to do good. Freedom at retirement is the opportunity to take on different responsibilities that will bless others.

Proverbs 3:27

⚡ POWER POINT: Although you may toss your Day Timer™ in the garbage, keep a calendar handy to plan out some special things to do to bless others. Try and do at least one each week.

CHAPTER TWENTY

SOME RETIREMENT DEFINITIONS

Fifty years ago when a person said something about retiring, they were usually talking about going to bed.

Nowadays, 65 is the age when one acquires sufficient experience to lose his/her job. Mandatory retirement can be another form of compulsory poverty if we're ill prepared, but retirement can be a great joy if you can figure how to prepare for it.

Today, "retirement security" is making sure all the doors are locked before you go to bed. The key to a happy retirement is to have enough money to live on but not enough to have to worry about.

One wife's humorous definition of retirement is: "Twice as much husband and only half as much income."

And, now, let's read a humorous tidbit from the life of Carl Johnson of Kankakee, Illinois:

"My wife and I took our grandchildren to visit my parents in Missouri. When we were ready to leave, my dad gave me a picture of myself. I had sent it to my parents during the second World War. I was dressed in my complete army uniform on which I had pinned my medals. As I walked out the door and into the yard, Amy, my five-year-old granddaughter, asked, "Who is that? Papa, is that you?"

I answered, "Yes, that is a picture of me."

Then she asked, "Did you fight in the war?"

I replied, "Yes, I fought in the war."

When we arrived home, my daughter and son-in-law came to get the children. Amy was still excited, she could hardly wait to tell her parents about her war hero grandfather. She grabbed the picture and ran to her mother. Excitedly, she said, "Mother, I think I know something you don't know. Did you know that Papa fought in the Civil War?"

Okay...so what is the bottom line? Many fine Christians have been taught to study, know, proclaim, and practice the Word of God, yet they ignore all the seniors who are described in it who have done mighty things for God. For example, Moses was 80 years old when he embarked on leading the Israelites from Egypt. Today people in America think seniors are only scarred, cracked, chipped, crumbled, and broken antiques of no value so they set them aside. However, most other societies honor and value their elders.

Don't let anyone put you down because you're a senior! You have great value; you still have much to contribute. Begin with reaching out to any grandkids or neighbor kids you may have, or minister to those "really old" folks who could use a kind smile or a heart-felt prayer from you.

Psalm 92:12a, 14-15

⚡ POWER POINT: Success in life seems to be largely a matter of hanging on long after others have let go. Let's hang in there even if they think we fought in the Civil War.

CHAPTER TWENTY-ONE

WHAT'S MOST IMPORTANT

In 1926, Johnny Sylvester was kicked in the head by a horse. The wound on his forehead became badly infected, and he was hospitalized. The doctors told his parents the sad news that there was no hope and that Johnny would soon die.

Johnny had one last wish that he told to his parents and the medical staff at the hospital. "I wish I could see Babe Ruth wallop a homer before I die."

So a telegram was then sent to the great slugger of the New York Yankees. The Babe sent back a telegram in answer to this young boy's dying wish. He promised to hit a homer just for Johnny in the next baseball game and that Johnny should be listening on the radio to hear it happen.

Johnny Sylvester, almost overnight became one of the most famous boys in baseball history. The newspapers of the day and the radio news services picked up the story, and featured it. Did Babe Ruth hit a homer for Johnny in that next game?

Yes! He did! Actually, he hit three homers in that particular game! Then, to top it all off, later, the great slugger visited Johnny in the hospital, which became quite an event with all of the media also present.

Were the doctors right? Did Johnny die? Yes…they were right. Johnny Sylvester—the critically ill youngster,—eventually died, but it was in 1990 when he had reached the ripe age of 74.

The following is a most interesting tribute given by Babe Ruth about the life of a minister whom he knew and had observed during his youth.

"Most of the people who have really counted in my life were not famous. Nobody ever heard of them, except those who knew and loved them. I knew an old minister once. His hair was white; his face shone. I have written my name on thousands of baseballs in my life. The old minister wrote his name on just a few simple hearts. How I envy him. Because he was not trying to please his own immortal soul, fame never came to him. I am listed as a famous home-runner, yet beside that obscure minister, who was so good and so wise, I never got to first base." (*The Civic Bulletin*)

What really is important in life? Too often we let the "urgent" push out the "really important," in spite of the fact that life doesn't go on forever. There comes a time when we will die and following this final event in life, there will be an accounting of how we have lived this life before the Judge of the universe. At that moment, the "urgents" of life will seem unimportant. What will be really important is to hear the longed for, "Well done, good and faithful servant."

Hebrews 9:27

POWER POINT: What we might think is the beginning may in reality be the end...and what we view as the end might just be a whole new beginning. It just might be possible to start all over again because many things in life are not at all what they might appear to be. Why not sit down and think about what you might begin today.

CHAPTER TWENTY-TWO

THE BEGGAR KING

Once there was a time, according to this legend, when Ireland was ruled by a king who had no son or grandson, which meant in those days that he therefore had no heirs. The king sent couriers to post notices in all the towns of his realm, advising every qualified young man to apply for an interview with him to determine if they could be a possible successor to the throne. However, all candidates had to have two qualifications. They must: 1) Love God and 2) Love fellow human beings.

The young man about whom this legend centers saw the notice and reflected that he loved God and also his neighbors. Only one thing stopped him from applying—he was so poor that he had no clothes that would make him presentable in the sight of the king. Neither did he have the funds to purchase the provisions needed for the long journey to the castle. So the young man begged here and borrowed there and worked at odd jobs until he managed enough for appropriate clothes and some provisions for the long journey.

Properly attired, the young man set out on his journey and had almost reached the castle when he came upon a poor beggar by the roadside. The beggar was pitiful, trembling, and dressed in tattered rags. With arms extended the beggar pleaded for help, "I'm hungry and I'm cold. Please, please help me...please?"

This young man was so touched by the beggar's plight that he immediately took off his new clothes and exchanged them with the tattered rags of the beggar. Without any kind of hesitation, he also gave him all the provisions he had left.

Now, somewhat hesitant, he continued on his way to the castle, dressed in the rags of the beggar and with no provisions for his walk back home. When he arrived, one of the king's attendants met him in the great hall of the castle. After cleaning off some of the grime from the beggar's old clothes, he was finally admitted to the throne room where the king sat.

The young man bowed in reverence. When he looked up, he gasped in astonishment. "You...it's you! *You* were the beggar by the road."

"Yes," the king replied with a smile. "I was that beggar."

"But...bu...buu...you were a beggar. You are the real king!? Why..." he finally managed to stammer out after gaining some of his composure.

"Because this was my test to every young man on his way to the castle. I had to find out if any of the young men really loved God and their fellow human beings," replied the king. "If we met as we are now, I would never really know if you cared enough about others. So I used this trick, and through it I found that you are the only one who helped the begger. I have discovered that you really do care and are the only one who sincerely loves God and others. You will become my son. You will be the next king, my successor to this throne. You will inherit my entire kingdom!"

John 13:34-35

POWER POINT: How do we become more loving? The closer we come to God, who is defined like this: "God is love," the closer we come to be a loving person in our relationships with others.

CHAPTER TWENTY-THREE

YOU ARE BLESSED

Ever feel that you have been cheated and don't have what you deserve? Let's look at things from another perspective.

If you own inspirational books and a Bible, you are abundantly blessed because one third of this world does not have access to even one.

If you woke up this morning with more good health than sickness, you are more blessed than the million who will not survive this week.

If you have never experienced the danger of battle, the loneliness of imprisonment, the agony of torture, or the pangs of starvation, you are ahead of more than 500 million people around this world.

If you attend church without fear of harassment, arrest, torture or even death, you are more blessed than almost three billion people in the world.

If you have food in your refrigerator, clothes on your back, a roof over your head, and a place to sleep, you are richer than 75% of this world's population.

If you have money in the bank, in your wallet or purse, and spare change in a dish someplace, you are among the top 8% of the world's wealthy.

If your parents are still alive and married, if your children are alive and still married, if your grandchildren are alive and still married, you are very rare and blessed...even in these United States.

If you hold up your head high with a smile on your face and are truly thankful, you are blessed because, although the majority of people you meet could, most do not.

If you can hold someone's hand, touch them on a shoulder, or hug them, you are blessed because you can offer God's healing touch through your love and compassion.

If you prayed today or yesterday, you are in the minority of those blessed because you believe in the reality of a God who is willing to hear your prayers and answer them in response to your faith.

If you can read this message, you are more blessed than over two billion people in the world who cannot read anything at all.

How blessed we all are! The words containing the word "bless" are found approximately 550 times in the Bible! We read about the blessings of the father to his children that was passed along in many of the stories in the Old Testament. Today, we have the opportunity to pass along our blessings to others, beginning right in our own families with our children and grandchildren.

It is God's will to bless us and other significant people in our lives not because we happen to be such a wonderful people, but because it is in His very nature to bless. God does not love us nor does He bless us because of what we do or not do. (That's legalism and we have been freed from such bondage. However, some of God's blessings are conditional and subject to obedience on our part.) But God blesses us because He has chosen to do so, as we must choose to do with the people He has placed in our lives. When we are blessed, this blessing is to be passed along to others beginning with our family members.

Genesis 12:2-3

⚡ POWER POINT: It's important to take some time and count our many blessings. Why are we blessed? It's a "God thing" to bless. But after we are blessed, we need to pass it along to somebody so that they, too, can experience the blessing. How many blessings have you passed along recently? How many can you do next month?

CHAPTER TWENTY-FOUR

WHAT IS A BIBLICAL BLESSING?

A bearded old man once patted the head of Leo Rosten when he was ten years old, chuckled fondly and said, "You look like a nice boy. I bless you with long life so you should live to a 121."

Later, when he told his father, Leo's father explained, "Jews say that because Moses lived to be 120."

"Oh, but why did the old man tell me 121?"

Rosten's father smiled, "Maybe he didn't want you to die suddenly."

What is a "biblical blessing"? It's the impartation of the supernatural power of God into another human life as spoken by a delegated authority of God. Its purpose is to make holy, consecrate, honor, endow, affirm, encourage, build up, invoke favor, or show high regard.

This is an action which has largely been lost to the Church for the past 2000 years or more, but it is still practiced by the Jewish people. It's a concept created by God, "God created man in his own image, in the image of God he created him; male and female he created them. God blessed them and said to them…" (Genesis 1:27-28a).

Words have life, meaning and power! When spoken by a designated authority they can literally shape the destiny of another. The Jewish people have practiced this principle of impartation since the days of Abraham. Each Sabbath, as part of their worship, Jewish parents bless their children in the name of the God of Abraham, Isaac, and Jacob. When boys reach the age of thirteen and girls turn twelve, there is a very special blessing ceremony, called a *bat mitzvah* for girls and a *bar mitzvah* for boys. Before the congregation their parents place their hands on them and pronounce the blessing on their lives. (Grandparents and rabbis are also participants.)

They are speaking words into young lives that can shape their futures and destinies. Parents and grandparents bless them, and these blessed children, in turn, are expected to go out into the world and become a blessing to others.

Contrast that practice to the Gentile neighbors across the street who are telling their kids, "You're stupid; you'll never amount to anything!" By the words we say we can bless or curse children. When a negative is spoken to a child, according to my wife who is a counseling psychologist, it takes 47 positive words to overcome the negative one!

Jesus began his ministry by pronouncing nine special blessings in His "Sermon on the Mount," which today we call "The Beatitudes." He concluded his ministry with a blessing (Matthew 5:3-12; Luke 24:50-51). During His ministry He often blessed the children as He touched them or picked them up and put his hands on them and pronounced blessings upon them.

The first and last priority of the ministry of Jesus was marked by the blessings He pronounced on others. If He did it, why can't we do the same? He is our example and life pattern. Paul the Apostle, the writer of a number of New Testament epistles, concluded each one with a blessing on his readers. We are commanded to bless others and not curse them. This is one powerful life motivator!

Mark 10:14

⚡ POWER POINT: As a grandparent...why don't you begin periodically blessing your grandkids. This can take place on a casual level or it can become something special with lots of advance planning. Try it and you might be surprised at what happens.

CHAPTER TWENTY-FIVE

WHO YOU ARE MAKES THE DIFFERENCE

A teacher in New York decided to honor each of her seniors in high school by telling them what difference they each made. Using a process developed by Helice Bridges of Del Mar, California, she called each student to the front of the class, one at a time. First she told them how the student made a difference to her and the class. Then she presented each of them with a blue ribbon imprinted in gold letters, which read: "WHO I AM MAKES A DIFFERENCE."

Then this teacher decided to take this one step further as a class project to see what kind of an impact such a recognition could have on their community. She gave each of her students three more ribbons and instructed them to go out and spread this acknowledgment ceremony, first by giving one out recognizing someone they knew and giving the recipient the other two to pass out in turn. The students were to follow up on the results and see who honored whom and report back to the class in a week.

One of the students went to a junior executive in a nearby company and honored the man for helping him with his career planning. He gave him the blue ribbon and also passed along the two extra ribbons and said, "We're doing a class project on recognition, and we'd like you to go out and find somebody to honor. First, honor them by giving them a blue ribbon for themselves, and then give them the extra ribbon to pass along so they can acknowledge someone else. Then, please report back to me and tell me what happened."

Later that day, the junior executive went to his boss who was a notoriously grouchy kind of man. He sat his boss down and told him he deeply admired him for being a creative genius. The boss was surprised and pleased, and then the junior executive asked him to acknowledge someone else with the remaining ribbon.

That night, the boss came home to his fourteen-year-old son and said: "The most incredible thing happened to me today. One of the junior executives came in and told me he admired me and gave me a blue ribbon for being a creative genius. Imagine! As I was driving home, I started thinking about whom I would honor with this other ribbon and I thought about you. I want to honor you. My days are hectic, and when I come home, I often don't pay attention to you. Sometimes I scream at you for not getting good grades or leaving your room in a mess, but somehow, tonight, I just want to sit here and let you know that you do make a difference for me. Besides your mother, you are the most important person in my life. You're a great kid, and I love you!"

The startled boy started to sob and sob and couldn't stop crying. His whole body shook. He looked up through his tears and said, "I was planning to commit suicide tomorrow, Dad, because I didn't think you loved me. Now I don't need to." (Helice Bridges, Chairperson of the "Board for Difference Makers" Inc., Del Mar, CA, condensed and adapted).

Virginia Satir wrote: "We need four hugs a day for survival. We need eight hugs a day for maintenance. We need twelve hugs a day for growth."

Proverbs 3:27

⚡ POWER POINT: It's such a little thing, but what an impact a few words of love for another will do! Kids are so vulnerable and so needy in this area. It's time we are the vehicle of the love they so desperately need. What a difference it makes! Just say it and let your actions confirm it!

CHAPTER TWENTY-SIX

ENTHUSIASTIC TEACHING

Howard Hendricks tells of an 83-year-old woman that he and some other conference leaders happened to have lunch with during a Sunday School Convention at the Moody Church in Chicago. In the course of conversation it was learned that she was a teacher of 13 junior-high boys in a church, which averaged 55 attendees. She was asked why she was attending the conference. Here's her story:

"I'm on a pension; my husband died a number of years ago," she replied, "and, frankly this is the first time a convention has come close enough to my home so I could afford to attend. I bought a Greyhound ticket and rode all night to get here this morning and attend two workshops. I want to learn something that will make me a better teacher."

Hendricks said, "I couldn't help thinking about all the frauds across America who would be breaking their arms patting themselves on the back if they had 13 boys in a Sunday School of 55 and thinking to themselves, 'Who, me go to a Sunday School convention? Man, I can tell them how to do it!' Not this woman."

Hendricks also added, "I heard a sequel to this story some time later. A doctor told me there are 84 young men in or moving toward Christian ministry as a result of this woman's influence."

In fact, a number of them were in the seminary where Hendricks was a professor. Hendricks asked two of them, "What do you remember most about her?"

They replied, "She is the most unforgettable person we've ever met. She's still going hard; fills her car with kids and brings them to church." (Howard Hendricks, *Say It With Love*, Victor Books, adapted)

Awesome! This kind of a productive life is a challenge to all of us! Too many aging Christians assume that they are in a red-light situation, waiting for the light to turn green. Let's assume, instead, that we are in a green-light situation, and going strong until we see the red-light. It's really all a matter of perspective as to how serious we are about making what time we have left in our life something that makes an impact. It's never too late!

Let's combine that challenge with this interesting fact. Look at the name of "God"; two-thirds of that name is "Go." And if you turn that around, by the same kind of logic, two-thirds of God's name is "Do." Therefore the "gospel" is "go and do in God's name!" Let's put the go and the do back into our living.

Words aren't enough. Praying isn't enough. It's "going and doing" with the message of the good news balanced with living a lifestyle which backs up what we say. Really, people are not very interested in what we have to say, anyway—people want to see this message put into action. In other words, we need to live out the principles we share. Go and do, beginning with children, grandchildren, neighbors, and friends. It's never too late to start.

As I read the Bible I cannot find anything about this life-ending event which we call "retirement." As I see it, we are to go out in a blaze of glory. We are to end strong. We are to take a final lap before we break the finish line. We must continue to live even when the end in sight. There is a reward waiting for all who are consistent and faithful to the end. What fabulous words of reward will be heard, "Well done, good and faithful servant. Enter into the joys of your Lord!"

Mark 16:15

POWER POINT: Why not sit down and make a plan of how to do those things that God has shown you are important to Him.

ABOUT THE AUTHOR

Robert Strand is the author of more than 57 books, and his "Moments to Give" series has sold more than a million copies. A consummate story-teller, Robert knows how to blend the emotional impact of true stories with practical insights from his many years of pastoral experience to produce break-through results. To this end, he has written six other books in the Power Book series.

He and his wife Donna live in Springfield, Missouri.

Note: the answer to the riddle on page 62 is the whale from the book of Jonah.

Other books by Robert Strand
From Evergreen Press:

The Power of Forgiving
True stories and practical instruction to help you deal with irritations, heal relational breaks, and forgive the "unforgivable."
ISBN 1-58169-050-9 96 p $5.99

The Power of Thanksgiving
Time to take inventory of your blessings and begin a new lifestyle of thanksgiving.
ISBN 1-58169-054-1 96 p $5.99

The Power of Gift Giving
Learn how to give the intangible parts of your life and become a source of blessing to others.
ISBN 1-58169-055-X 96 p $5.99

The Power of Motherhood
Mothers have a unique job nurturing kids today, but Strand shares stories, Scripture, and teaching that encourage mothers to be all they can be.
ISBN 1-58169-094-0 96 p $5.99

The Power of Fatherhood
Fathers have a challenging job raising kids in today's turbulent times, but Robert Strand shares over 20 stories that speak to the father's heart.
ISBN 1-58169-095-9 96 p $5.99

The Power of Debt-Free Living
Biblical principles on which to build a sound financial future are displayed through 20 true stories.
ISBN 1-58169-101-7 96 p. $5.99